GLUTEN FREE OVEN MADE DINNER RECIPES

by Renae Welsh

Table of Contents

CHICKEN:
Herb and Goat Cheese Chicken Breasts 5

Baked Almond Flour Chicken Nuggets 8

Spaghetti Squash Chicken Carbonara 11

Garlic and Rosemary Cornish Game Hens 14

Baked Lemon Chicken 17

Chicken Enchilada Casserole 20

Rosemary and Garlic Chicken 23

Texas Ranch Chicken 26

Italian Style Chicken Thighs 28

TURKEY:
Turkey and Vegetable Casserole 31

Turkey Meatballs 35

Turkey Spaghetti Pie 38

BEEF:
Insanely Easy Cheeseburger Pie 44

Crowd Pleasing Taco Tater Tots 47

Stuffed Green Peppers 50

Spiky Meatballs 53

Gluten Free Meatza 55

Dead Easy Pasta Casserole 58

Topsy Turvy Pizza 60

Creamy Cheesy Casserole 63

Meaty Roll Ups 66

Simple, Amazing Rib Roast 68

LAMB:
Cumin and Garlic Leg of Lamb 71
Rosemary Roast Leg of Lamb 74

PORK:
Impossibly Easy Breakfast Bake..77
Italian Sausage and Spaghetti Squash Casserole............................80
Bacon and Egg Quiche Lorraine..83
Italian Seasoned Pork Tenderloin...86
Bacon and Three Cheese Macaroni..89
Mexican Chorizo Bake 92
Sausage and Pepperoni Pizza Bake 95

FISH:
Simple Tuna Noodle Casserole...98
Garlic Baked Tilapia 101

VEGETARIAN:
Individual Portobello Pizzas..103
Quinoa Crusted Quiche 105
Quinoa Meatless Frittatas 107
Spicy Macaroni and Cheese 110
Italian 3 Cheese Eggplant Lasagna 113
Lasagna Style Zucchini Parmesan Bake 117

Copyright © 2017 by Renae Welsh

All rights reserved. No part of this publication may be reproduced, distributed, or transmitted in any form or by any means, including photocopying, recording, or other electronic or mechanical methods, without the prior written permission of the publisher, except in the case of brief quotations embodied in critical reviews and certain other noncommercial uses permitted by copyright law.

Herb and Goat Cheese Chicken Breasts

This chicken breast dish is easy to make, packed with protein, and uses just 7 ingredients! It is a wonderful comfort food that can be paired with any vegetable or starch (or both!) of your choice. I recommend mashed potatoes and green beans or sweet peas.

Preparation Time: 10 minutes
Cook Time: 25 minutes
Total Time: 35 minutes

Ingredients

2 small skinless, boneless chicken breast halves
2 ½ tablespoons of fresh goat cheese
1 pinch of dried parsley
1 pinch of garlic powder
1 pinch of dried oregano
1 pinch of dried thyme
Salt to taste

Directions

Preheat oven to 375 degrees Fahrenheit.

Line a baking sheet with non-stick aluminum foil.

Stir goat cheese and all spices together in a bowl until well blended, set aside.

Bake chicken breasts in the oven for 15 minutes.

After 15 minutes, remove the chicken breasts from the oven and spread the goat cheese with herbs mixture over the top of each breast.

Return chicken to oven, continuing to cook for 5-10 minutes or until there is no pink in the center (an instant-read thermometer can be used – the chicken should be at least 165 degrees Fahrenheit in the middle).

Remove chicken from oven, let rest for 2 minutes.

Serve and enjoy!

Baked Almond Flour Chicken Nuggets

Chicken nuggets are a favorite of children everywhere, but the grain-filled batter leaves a lot to be desired nutrition wise. These chicken nuggets are completely gluten-free because they use almond flour, and with the addition of some delicious spices, Mom and Dad will love these as much as the kids!

Preparation Time: 20 minutes
Cooking Time: 10 minutes
Total Time: 35 minutes

Ingredients

1 ¼ pounds of ground chicken
2 cups of King Arthur Almond Flour
¼ cup of cornstarch
¼ cup of water
2 tablespoons of olive oil
2 teaspoons of salt (divided)
2 teaspoons of ground black pepper (divided)
½ teaspoon of dry mustard
½ teaspoon of paprika

½ teaspoon of dried oregano

Directions

Preheat oven to 375 degrees Fahrenheit.

Place an oven-safe wire rack on top of a baking sheet and set aside.

Combine chicken, 1 teaspoon each of the salt and pepper, plus the dry mustard, paprika, and dried oregano in a large mixing bowl.

In a separate mixing bowl, whisk the almond flour and the remaining salt and pepper.

In a third mixing bowl, whisk together the cornstarch and cold water (the result will be thick).

With wet hands, form about 2 tablespoons of chicken into a small disk shape.

Coat the chicken disk in almond flour, then dip it into the cornstarch mix, then coat it again with the almond flour and then place it on the wire rack on top of a baking sheet.

Repeat the above process until all chicken has been coated with almond flour.

In a non-stick skillet, heat the 2 teaspoons of olive oil.

When the olive oil is hot, add half of the chicken nuggets to the pan, cooking for just 1 minute on each side (you just want to brown each side, not cook the chicken).

Repeat the above process until all the nuggets are browned.

Place all of the nuggets back on the wire rack on top of a baking sheet.

Place the baking sheet with wire rack in the oven on the center rack, and bake for 10 minutes.

Remove nuggets from the oven and flip them over on the rack.

Allow nuggets to cool on the wire rack for several minutes.

Serve with your favorite dipping sauce and enjoy!

Spaghetti Squash Chicken Carbonara

This recipe is not only gluten free, it is also high in protein, low fat, and low carbohydrate! By substituting spaghetti squash for pasta, and adding in just a little bacon, this casserole is sure to please even the pickiest of eaters in your family.

Preparation Time: 15 minutes
Cooking Time: 1 hour, 15 minutes
Total Time: 1 hour, 30 minutes

Ingredients

1 pound of chopped, cooked chicken (I recommend chicken breast)
14 ounces of shredded Parmesan cheese
1 spaghetti squash, halved and seeded

6 large eggs
1 can (12 ounces) of evaporated milk
1 bunch of green onions, chopped
1 tablespoon of garlic powder
1 tablespoon of salt
1 tablespoon of dried oregano
¼ cup of bacon bits
Ground black pepper to taste

Directions

Preheat oven to 375 degrees Fahrenheit, and line a baking sheet with parchment paper.

Place both halves of the spaghetti squash face down onto the baking sheet.

Bake the spaghetti squash until the flesh is tender, 30 to 45 minutes (test with a fork).

Remove spaghetti squash from oven, and allow several minutes for it to cool so it can be handled.

Scrape the flesh of the squash from the rind into a large bowl with a fork.

In a separate bowl, whisk eggs, evaporated milk, garlic powder, and oregano.

Pour the egg, milk, and spice mixture over the squash.

In a separate bowl, mix the chicken, bacon bits, black pepper, ½ of the parmesan cheese, and ½ of the green onions with the squash flesh.

With everything now combined, pour it all into a 9x13 casserole dish. Spread evenly.

Top the casserole with the remaining parmesan cheese and green onions.

Bake until the casserole is cooked through, about 45 minutes.

Remove dish from oven and allow a few minutes to cool.

Serve and enjoy!

Garlic and Rosemary Cornish Game Hens

This recipe makes for one flavorful bird, and everyone will think you slaved in the kitchen all day! There is just the right amount of spices to go with the white wine sauce, and the lemon and rosemary cook right into the chicken, giving it an exquisite taste. Baste the hens in their own juices every 10 minutes or so, and they will turn out wonderfully juicy.

Preparation Time: 20 minutes
Cook Time: 1 hour
Total Time: 1 hour, 20 minutes

Ingredients

4 Cornish game hens
8 sprigs of fresh rosemary
3 tablespoons of olive oil
24 cloves of garlic
1/3 cup of white wine
1/3 cup of chicken broth
1 lemon, quartered
Salt, to taste

Pepper, to taste

Directions

Preheat oven to 450 degrees Fahrenheit.

Rub all 4 hens with 1 tablespoon of olive oil, and lightly season with salt and pepper.

Place 1 lemon wedge and 1 sprig of rosemary in the cavity of each hen.

Put all 4 hens in a large roasting pan, and place all the garlic cloves around the hens.

Cook hens in the oven for 25 minutes.

Reduce oven temperature to 350 degrees Fahrenheit.

In a large mixing bowl, whisk together wine, chicken broth, the remaining 2 tablespoons of olive oil, and pour this mixture over the hens.

Continue roasting the hens for roughly 25 more minutes, or until they are golden brown and juices run clear. Baste the hens with pan juices about every 10 minutes.

Move hens to a platter, pouring any cavity juices back into the roasting pan.

Tent the hens with aluminum foil to keep them warm.

Transfer pan juices and garlic cloves into a medium saucepan and boil until the liquid turns into a sauce, roughly 6 minutes.

Cut hens in half lengthwise, and arrange on plates.

Spoon sauce and garlic around hens.

Garnish with the 4 remaining rosemary sprigs, serve, and enjoy!

Baked Lemon Chicken

Cooking an entire chicken is an economical way to serve a very tasty and filling dinner, as you pay a lot more per pound for the convenience of having individual cuts of breasts, thighs, drumsticks, etc. This recipe mixes Italian seasoning (the kind that comes in a packet) with fresh lemon juice to give it a great zestiness.

Preparation Time: 15 minutes
Cooking Time: 1 hour, 30 minutes
Total Time: 1 hour, 45 minutes

Ingredients

1 whole chicken (3 pounds)
2 lemons
2 tablespoons of olive oil
2 teaspoons of Italian seasoning
½ teaspoon of seasoning salt
½ teaspoon of mustard powder
1 teaspoon of garlic powder

½ teaspoon of ground black pepper

Directions

Preheat oven to 350 degrees Fahrenheit.

Mix together the Italian seasoning, salt, mustard powder, garlic powder and black pepper in a small bowl.

Rinse the chicken thoroughly and remove the giblets.

Place chicken in a 9x13 baking dish.

Sprinkle 1 ½ teaspoons of the spice mixture (mixed in the second step) inside the chicken.

Rub the remaining spice mixture on the outside of the chicken.

Squeeze the juice of 2 lemons into a small bowl, and mix with the olive oil.

Drizzle the olive oil and lemon juice mixture over the whole chicken.

Bake chicken for 1 ½ hours, or until juices run clear, basting several times with the remaining oil mixture.

Allow to cool for several minutes before carving.

Serve and enjoy!

Chicken Enchilada Casserole

This satisfying casserole gives you all the flavor of your favorite Mexican restaurant chicken enchiladas without any of the wheat! By using a gluten free cornbread mix, you get a very flavorful meal all in one pan with just 15 minutes of preparation work. While I recommend using King Arthur Gluten Free Cornbread mix, you can use any brand you would like – just make sure it is plain cornbread and not honey cornbread.

Preparation Time: 15 minutes
Cook Time: 45 minutes
Total time: 1 hour

Ingredients

1 pound of chicken breast tenderloins
½ box (7.5 ounce) of King Arthur Gluten Free cornbread mix
1 egg
1/3 cup of milk
1 can (15 ounces) of tomato sauce

¼ cup of water
1 envelope of taco seasoning mix
1 can (15 ounces) of black beans, drained
1 cup of shredded Mexican-style cheese blend
¼ cup of cream cheese
1 ½ tablespoons of chili powder
1 tablespoon of vegetable oil

Directions

Preheat oven to 375 degrees Fahrenheit.

Grease a 9x9 baking dish.

In a saucepan, mix together chili powder, taco seasoning mix, tomato sauce, and water, and bring to a simmer over medium heat.

Heat oil in a skillet over medium heat, then brown the chicken tenderloins on both sides (about 5 minutes per side).

Pour tomato sauce mix over the chicken, bring to a simmer, then continue cooking over medium-low heat until the chicken is no longer pink on the inside (about 8 minutes).

Shred cooked chicken in a bowl, then return chicken to the saucepan with the tomato sauce.

Mix black beans and cream cheese in with chicken and sauce until thoroughly combined.

Pour entire mixture into baking dish and top with Mexican cheese.

Whisk corn bread mix, milk, and egg in a bowl, then spoon this batter over the chicken mix.

Bake until the casserole is bubbling and the corn bread topping is browned (about 30 minutes).

Rosemary and Garlic Chicken

What can make a whole baked chicken with lemon and rosemary even better? Why, add butter, of course! You infuse the chicken by stuffing the sauce mixture in between the meat and the skin. All the seasoning penetrates both the meat and skin this way, so you get amazing flavor with every bite.

Preparation Time: 15 minutes
Cook Time: 45 minutes
Total time: 1 hour

Ingredients

1 (3 pound) whole chicken
1 large lemon
5 cloves of garlic, sliced
5 sprigs of fresh rosemary
¼ cup of chopped fresh rosemary
1 cup of unsalted butter, softened
3 tablespoons of garlic, minced
1 teaspoon of paprika
Salt to taste
Black pepper to taste

Directions

Preheat oven to 350 degrees Fahrenheit.

Rinse the chicken and pat it dry.

Grate the lemon peel all over to get lemon zest.

Slice the lemon into quarters and set aside.

Using a hand mixer, combine the butter, lemon zest, minced garlic, and ¼ cup chopped fresh rosemary.

Create pockets around the chicken by sliding your fingers in between the meat and skin on the breast, as well as between the leg and wing joints.

Stuff the butter mixture into the pockets you have created, but save about ¼ of the butter mixture.

Take the remaining butter mixture and rub it on the inside of the chicken.

Turn the chicken on its rear, with the open neck facing upward, and sprinkle the cavity with the salt, pepper, and paprika. Add in the quartered lemon, rosemary sprigs, and sliced garlic cloves to the cavity.

Bind the chicken's legs with culinary twine, and tuck the wings into the leg joints.

Place the chicken, breast up, onto a roasting rack and into the oven.

Roast the chicken for approximately 50 minutes, or until juices run clear.

Removing stuffing, carve the chicken, serve, and enjoy!

Texas Ranch Chicken

This insanely simple recipe infuses ranch flavors all while keeping the chicken nice and moist, then you top it with cheese to make it creamy and delicious. You can even play up the recipe to your own liking, for example you can use a packet of ranch dressing mix (as pictured above), and sour cream in place of the bottled dressing.

Preparation Time: 10 minutes
Cook Time: 35 minutes
Total time: 45 minutes

Ingredients

1 ½ pounds of boneless, skinless chicken (I suggest breasts and/or thighs)
1 ½ cups of bottled Ranch salad dressing
2 cups of shredded mozzarella cheese
2 teaspoons of olive oil

Directions

Preheat oven to 350 degrees Fahrenheit.

Coat the inside of a 9x13 baking dish with the olive oil.

Place chicken pieces in dish close together so that the cheese and dressing do not burn at the bottom.

Bake for 20 minutes.

Remove from oven, top the chicken with the mozzarella cheese, then return to the oven.

Continue baking for about 15 minutes, or until the cheese is melted and slightly brown and the chicken is no longer pink.

Serve and enjoy!

Italian Style Chicken Thighs

Slow cooking these chicken thighs for over an hour lets the Italian inspired sauce really soak in to the meat without drying it out. Note that you can use any vegetables you'd like (potatoes, carrots and tomatoes are in the picture above), and putting the garlic and onion through a food processor makes it that much easier to have a smooth sauce.

Preparation Time: 15 minutes
Cook Time: 1 hour, 15 minutes
Total time: 1 hour, 30 minutes

Ingredients

15 chicken thighs
8 large potatoes, peeled and quartered
10 cloves of garlic, crushed
1 onion, minced
1 cup of vegetable oil
½ cup of wine vinegar

5 lemons, juiced
2 tablespoons of dried oregano
2 tablespoons of dried parsley
Salt to taste
Pepper to taste

Directions

Preheat oven to 350 degrees Fahrenheit.

Place chicken pieces in a 10x15 inch enameled roasting pan.

Heat a large skillet over medium heat.

Fry the potatoes in ½ inch deep oil until golden brown, then put them around the chicken pieces in the roasting pan.

Mix together the wine vinegar, garlic, oregano, parsley, onion, lemon juice, salt and pepper with the remaining oil, then pour this mixture over the chicken and potatoes.

Bake for 1 ¼ hours, basting the chicken and potatoes with the sauce occasionally.

Remove from oven and let rest for approximately 5 minutes.

Serve and enjoy!

Turkey and Vegetable Casserole

This casserole is heavy on the veggies, but they are masked by all the cheese, seasonings, and ground turkey – so it's perfect for picky young eaters! The best part is that just about any vegetables can be substituted in the recipe, so you can have fun experimenting with this one.

Preparation Time: 25 minutes
Cook Time: 45 minutes
Total time: 1 hour, 20 minutes

Ingredients

1 ½ pounds of ground turkey
2 cups of fresh green beans, chopped
2 fresh zucchini, chopped
2 cups of crushed tomatoes
1 small onion, chopped very fine
1 cup of frozen peas
1 cup of fresh mushrooms, chopped
5 cloves of garlic, minced
1 teaspoon of extra-virgin olive oil

2 tablespoons of fresh basil, chopped
2 teaspoons of fresh thyme, chopped
2 tablespoons of freshly grated Parmesan cheese
1 cup of shredded mozzarella cheese
8 cups of water
Salt to taste
Pepper to taste

Directions

Preheat oven to 350 degrees Fahrenheit.

In a large pot, bring the water to a boil.

Cook green beans until just softened (about 3 minutes), drain and set aside.

Heat the olive oil in a large skillet over medium-low heat. Cook onion in hot oil, stirring occasionally, until it is clear (about 3 to 5 minutes).

Crumble ground turkey into the skillet with the onion and increase the heat to medium-high.

Season the turkey generously with salt and pepper, and cook until the turkey is completely browned (about 7 to 10 minutes), stirring occasionally.

Reduce heat to medium and then stir the garlic, basil and thyme into the turkey and onion mixture. Cook, stirring occasionally, for about another 3 minutes.

Remove the turkey mixture from the skillet with a slotted spoon (for draining), and transfer it to a 9x13 casserole dish.

Preserve about 2 tablespoons of pan drippings for later use, and discard the rest.

Heat the 2 tablespoons of pan drippings in the same skillet over medium heat. Stir in the green beans, peas, mushrooms, and zucchini, and season with salt and pepper.

Cook the vegetable mixture, stirring occasionally, until it is hot (about 5 minutes).

Add the vegetable mixture to the casserole dish, and stir everything together until combined.

Pour crushed tomatoes over the casserole dish mixture.

Top everything with the mozzarella cheese evenly.

Sprinkle the Parmesan cheese over the mozzarella cheese.

Bake until cheese is melted and vegetables are tender (about 20 minutes).

Remove from oven and let rest for about 10 minutes.

Serve and enjoy!

Turkey Meatballs

Most meatballs use beef or pork, but this recipe cuts out the fat while leaving the flavor of your typical meatball. Many stores carry gluten free bread crumbs, some brands to look for are Glutino (found at Walmart), Schar, and Kinnikinnick. Stick some toothpicks in these babies, serve with multiple types of sauce, and they are a great crowd pleaser!

Preparation Time: 15 minutes
Cook Time: 30 minutes
Total time: 45 minutes

Ingredients
¾ pounds of ground turkey
½ pounds of chicken sausage (casings removed)
2/3 cups of Kinnikinnick Gluten Free bread crumbs
¼ cup of grated Parmesan cheese
1 egg, lightly beaten
3 tablespoons of fresh basil, chopped
3 tablespoons of milk
2 teaspoons of minced garlic

1 teaspoon of salt
½ teaspoon of ground black pepper

Directions

Preheat oven to 350 degrees Fahrenheit.

Line a baking sheet with parchment paper.

Combine the ground turkey, chicken sausage, gluten free bread crumbs, milk, garlic, Parmesan cheese, basil, salt, and pepper in a large bowl. Mix everything together gently with a fork until combined.

Drop the mixture by the spoonful (in roughly 1 ½ inch diameter balls) onto the baking sheet.

Bake in the oven until cooked completely and lightly browned (about 30 minutes).

Serve and enjoy!

Turkey Spaghetti Pie

This pie uses spaghetti squash instead of pasta, turkey sausage, and a ton of vegetables and spices to really make things flavorful. Make sure the applesauce is unsweetened, it is more to keep things moist than for the taste! You can also add mozzarella cheese (as pictured above) for a bit more of a creamy texture.

Preparation Time: 15 minutes
Cook Time: 1 hour, 30 minutes
Total time: 1 hour, 45 minutes

Ingredients

1 pound (16 ounces) of ground turkey sausage
1 large spaghetti squash, halved lengthwise and seeded
1 cup of pizza sauce of your choice
1 cup of chopped baby spinach leaves
3 eggs, beaten
½ cup of diced onion
½ cup of diced red bell pepper
¼ cup of unsweetened applesauce
1 teaspoon of dried basil
½ teaspoon of garlic powder
½ teaspoon of dried oregano

¼ teaspoon of ground black pepper

Directions

Preheat oven to 400 degrees Fahrenheit.

Arrange spaghetti squash halves on a baking sheet, cut side down.

Bake squash for about 25 minutes, then let cool until it can be safely touched.

Scoop out strands of squash with a spoon, and place them in an 8 inch square baking dish.

Reduce oven temperature to 350 degrees Fahrenheit.

Brown the turkey sausage and diced onion in a large skillet over medium high heat until sausage is crumbly and onion is clear (5 to 7 minutes).

Remove skillet from heat and mix in pizza sauce, peppers, applesauce, spinach, basil, garlic powder, oregano, and black pepper until thoroughly combined.

Spread the mixture from the skillet over the squash in the square baking dish.

Pour raw eggs over the mixture in the baking dish, then use your hands to squish everything together until combined.

Bake for about 1 hour, or until everything is bubbling and the eggs are thoroughly cooked.

Serve and enjoy!

Miniature Meatloaves

While this is not your everyday, "combine all the ingredients and throw it in the oven" meatloaf, these miniature meatloaves are definitely worth the effort. The vegetable puree adds a lot of flavor and gives the meatloaf a certain je ne sais quoi, all while aiding the egg to hold everything together without any gluten-filled breadcrumbs. If you do not have a stick blender handy, simply use an ordinary blender, so long as the puree does not fill the blender more than halfway.

Preparation Time: 35 minutes
Cook Time: 1 hour, 5 minutes
Total Time: 1 hour, 40 minutes

Ingredients

1 tablespoon of coconut oil
¾ cup of diced carrots
¾ cup of diced onion
1 cup of lightly packed fresh spinach leaves
3 cloves of chopped garlic
1 can (14.5 ounces) of fire-roasted diced tomatoes

1 large pinch of chopped fresh thyme
1 large pinch of chopped fresh parsley
2 2/3 pounds of lean ground beef (10% fat is recommended)
1 egg, lightly beaten
OPTIONAL: 3 slices of bacon, cut into 10 pieces
OPTIONAL: Your favorite ketchup

Directions

Preheat oven to 400 degrees Fahrenheit.

Line a baking sheet with non-stick foil.

Heat the coconut oil in a medium saucepan over medium heat.

Cook the carrots and onion in the hot oil, stirring frequently until softened (about 3 to 7 minutes – the onion will turn clear).

Add tomatoes, spinach, garlic, thyme, parsley, salt and pepper and bring to a simmer.

Reduce the heat to medium-low, and continue to simmer until the flavors combine (about 20 minutes).
Allow to cool for 5-10 minutes.

Puree the warm vegetables and spices with a stick blender until smooth.

Mix the pureed vegetables with the ground beef and egg together in a bowl with your hands or a wooden spoon until evenly combined.

Divide the meat/egg/vegetable mixture into 10 small meatloaves on the baking sheet.

OPTIONAL: Place 1 piece of bacon on each meatloaf.

Bake for 40 to 45 minutes, or until there is no pink in the center (an instant-read thermometer can be used – the meatloaves should be at least 160 degrees Fahrenheit in the center).

Remove meatloaves from the oven.

OPTIONAL: Top with your favorite ketchup.

Serve and enjoy!

Insanely Easy Cheeseburger Pie

Yummy, melty cheeseburgers are sadly something many people have to give up when going gluten free. There are gluten free hamburger buns available, but they are expensive and the texture often leaves a lot to be desired. This cheeseburger pie uses something I love to use: Bisquick® Gluten Free Mix!

Preparation Time: 15 minutes
Cook Time: 30 minutes
Total Time: 45 minutes

Ingredients

½ cup of Bisquick ® Gluten Free Mix
1 cup of milk
1 cup shredded cheddar cheese
3 large eggs
1 pound of lean (80% or higher) ground beef
1 medium onion, diced
½ teaspoon of salt
1/8 teaspoon of pepper

Directions

Preheat oven to 400 degrees Fahrenheit.

Grease a 9 inch glass pie plate with cooking spray or oil.

In a 10 inch skillet, brown the ground beef and onion over medium-high heat, stirring frequently until the beef is cooked and the onions are clear and soft.

Drain fat/grease from the skillet.

Stir salt and pepper in to ground beef and onion mix.

Spread the ground beef and onion mix into the pie plate, and sprinkle with the shredded cheese.

In a medium bowl, stir together the Bisquick Gluten Free mix, milk, and eggs until well blended.

Pour the contents of the bowl into the pie plate, on top of the ground beef and onion mix.

Bake the pie plate for 25-30 minutes, until a knife or toothpick inserted in the center comes out clean.

Serve and enjoy!

Crowd Pleasing Taco Tater Tots

These tater tots are sinfully delicious – definitely not a light meal, but a great crowd pleaser! This recipe takes a childhood favorite and grows them up a bit with ground beef, cream cheese, jalapenos or green onion, taco seasoning, and of course plenty of cheese! They are then served with sour cream for a flavor explosion. These are fantastic for gatherings, such as having people over for the big game.

Preparation Time: 15 minutes
Cook Time: 35 minutes
Total Time: 50 minutes

Ingredients

1 package (16 ounces) of frozen tater tots
1 pound of ground beef
1 ounce of processed cheese, such as Velveeta ®
1 package of taco seasoning mix
1 ounce of cream cheese
1 container of sour cream

1 can (4 ounces) of diced jalapeno peppers, or 4 ounces of diced green onions
1 can (15 ounces) of corn
1 jar (8 ounces) of salsa
4 ounces of shredded cheddar cheese
OPTIONAL: 1 can (4 ounces) of sliced black olives

Directions

Preheat oven to 400 degrees Fahrenheit.

Grease a 9 x 13" baking dish.

Heat a large skillet over medium-high heat.

Cook beef in skillet until browned, about 5 to 7 minutes, then drain grease/fat.

Add corn, salsa, processed cheese, cream cheese, and taco seasoning to the ground beef in the skillet, and stir until thoroughly blended together.

Spread entire mixture from skillet over the bottom of the baking dish.

Arrange tater tots over the beef mixture, and sprinkle cheddar cheese, jalapenos/green onion, and black olives (if you are using them) on top.

Bake for about 25 minutes, until tater tots are crispy and the cheese is bubbling.

Serve with sour cream and enjoy!

Stuffed Green Peppers

These stuffed peppers are a fantastically flavorful comfort food. By "gutting" the peppers, you take out most of the heat, but the spices and Worcestershire sauce add some zing back in. I use Mexican cheese to top off everything, but you can use any cheese you'd like...or none at all!

Preparation Time: 20 minutes
Cook Time: 1 hour
Total Time: 1 hour, 20 minutes

Ingredients

6 large green bell peppers
1 pound of ground beef
1 cup of water
½ cup of uncooked long grain white rice
½ cup of shredded Mexican cheese
2 (8 ounce) cans of tomato sauce
1 tablespoon of Worcestershire sauce
1 teaspoon of Italian seasoning
¼ teaspoon of garlic powder

¼ teaspoon of onion powder
Salt to taste
Pepper to taste

Directions

Preheat the oven to 350 degrees Fahrenheit.

Bring 1 cup of water to a boil in a saucepan, and add rice.

Reduce heat to simmer, cover the rice and cook for 20 minutes.

Brown the beef in a skillet over medium heat.

Cut off and throw out the tops, seeds, and innards of the bell peppers, hollowing them out.

Place the peppers in a baking dish with the open side facing upward (you may have to slice the bottoms so the peppers will stand upright).

In a separate bowl, mix the browned beef, cooked rice, 1 can of tomato sauce, Worcestershire sauce, garlic powder, onion powder, salt, and pepper together until evenly mixed.

Spoon the mixture into the bell peppers.

Mix the remaining can of tomato sauce and Italian seasoning in a separate bowl, then pour the sauce over the stuffed peppers.

Top with cheese as desired.

Bake for 1 hour, basting with sauce every 15 minutes, until the peppers are tender.

Serve and enjoy!

Spiky Meatballs

Often times called "porcupine meatballs," the rice is what gives them their rather spiky appearance! These freeze wonderfully, just heat them up in the oven later and serve with some mashed potatoes and corn.

Preparation Time: 30 minutes
Cook Time: 1 hour
Total Time: 1 hour, 30 minutes

Ingredients

1 pound of lean (at least 80%) ground beef
1 can (15 ounces) of tomato sauce
½ cup of uncooked long grain white rice
1 ½ cups of water
½ cup of diced onion
1 teaspoon of salt
½ teaspoon of celery salt
1/8 teaspoon of garlic powder

Directions

Preheat oven to 350 degrees Fahrenheit.

In a large bowl, mix together the ground beef, rice, ½ cup of water, and onion. Then blend in the salt, celery salt, garlic powder, and pepper until well mixed.

Shape the mixture from the bowl into 1.5" balls.

In a large skillet, brown the meatballs over medium heat. Drain fat.

In an 11x7 baking dish, mix together the tomato sauce and 1 cup of water.

Place meatballs in the tomato sauce, turning each meatball a few times to coat it in the sauce.

Cover the entire baking dish with foil.

Bake for 45 minutes.

Remove foil, then cook for another 15 minutes.

Serve and enjoy!

Gluten Free Meatza

This mock pizza is not only gluten free, but it is low carb and paleo! Who can resist a delicious pizza that has both ground beef and pepperoni, and 2 kinds of melted cheese? The recipe is for a basic pepperoni pizza, but it is expected that you add any other toppings you prefer – that is what pizza is all about! You can even do half and half with your toppings, as pictured.

Preparation Time: 30 minutes
Cook Time: 15 minutes
Total Time: 45 minutes

Ingredients
2 pounds of extra lean (90% or higher) ground beef
2 eggs
½ cup of grated Parmesan cheese
1 package (12 ounces) of shredded Mozzarella cheese
1 tablespoon of salt
1 teaspoon of dried oregano
1 teaspoon of garlic salt
1 teaspoon of ground black pepper
1 teaspoon of crushed red pepper flakes
1 cup of tomato sauce
1 package (3.5 ounces) of sliced pepperoni

Directions
Preheat oven to 450 degrees Fahrenheit.

Mix together the salt, oregano, garlic salt, ground black pepper, and crushed red pepper flakes in a small bowl.

In a separate, large bowl, mix together the ground beef and eggs until incorporated. Add Parmesan cheese and the seasoning mixture in the small bowl to the beef and combine.

Press the ground beef mixture into a 12x17 inch pan, and spread out evenly.

Bake in the oven until meat is no longer pink, about 10 minutes. Drain grease.

Set oven rack about 6 inches from the heat source, and turn on the oven's broiler.

Sprinkle roughly 1/3 of the Mozzarella cheese over the baked meat, then pour tomato sauce in an even layer over the meat and cheese.

Sprinkle another 1/3 of Mozzarella cheese over the sauce, then top with slices of pepperoni.

Sprinkle the remaining 1/3 of Mozzarella cheese over the entire pizza.

Broil until the cheese is melted and bubbling, about 3 to 5 minutes.

Serve and enjoy!

Dead Easy Pasta Casserole

This casserole is about as simple as you can get, with just 4 ingredients! The best part is that you can make it your own by adding chopped onion, black olives, different types of cheese – whatever your heart desires!

Preparation Time: 15 minutes
Cook Time: 25 minutes
Total Time: 40 minutes

Ingredients
1 pound of lean ground beef (85% or higher)
1 jar (28 ounces) of spaghetti sauce of your choice
1 box (16 ounces) of Barilla Gluten Free Rotini pasta
2 cups of shredded mozzarella cheese

Directions
Preheat oven to 350 degrees Fahrenheit.

Bring a large pot of water to a boil.

Add the pasta and cook, stirring occasionally, for 8 to 10 minutes until pasta is just becoming soft. Drain pasta and set aside.

In a large skillet, brown the ground beef over medium heat. Drain excess fat.

Add spaghetti sauce and pasta to browned beef in skillet.

In a three quart casserole dish, make layers alternating between the meat/pasta/sauce mixture and the mozzarella cheese, making sure that the top layer is cheese.

Bake casserole in oven for 25 minutes.

Serve and enjoy!

Topsy Turvy Pizza

This upside-down pizza dish (really a casserole) gives you a complete meal just like pizza does! You can add whatever toppings you would like before popping it in the oven, such as pepperoni, vegetables, pineapple, what have you. Just keep in mind that the "crust" consists of over a pound of ground beef, so it is pretty filling as it is!

Preparation Time: 15 minutes
Cook Time: 40 minutes
Total Time: 55 minutes

Ingredients

1 ½ pounds of lean ground beef (85% or higher)
1 can (15 ounces) of your choice of pizza sauce
1 yellow onion, chopped
2 cups of shredded mozzarella cheese
½ cup of shredded Italian blend cheese
1 cup of brown rice flour
1 cup of 2% milk
2 eggs
½ teaspoon of salt
¼ teaspoon of dried oregano

Directions

Preheat oven to 350 degrees Fahrenheit.

Grease a 9" x 13" baking dish and set aside.

Over medium-high heat, brown the beef and chopped onion in a large skillet until the beef is crumbled (roughly 5 to 7 minutes). Drain grease.

Stir pizza sauce and spices into the onion and ground beef mixture until thoroughly combined.

Spread the meat, onion, pizza sauce and spices mixture into the greased baking dish, then top evenly with the shredded mozzarella cheese.

In a medium mixing bowl, whisk together the eggs, milk, and brown rice flour until well mixed.

Spread the egg, milk and flour mixture over the layer of mozzarella cheese.

Evenly sprinkle the Italian cheese on top of the entire dish.

Bake until the cheese is bubbling, approximately 35 minutes.

Serve and enjoy!

Creamy Cheesy Casserole

This recipe uses cream cheese to make everything extra moist and – you guessed it – creamy! The Italian seasoning, red pepper flakes, onion and garlic also give it such amazing flavor, you will think you are eating from your favorite Italian restaurant.

Preparation Time: 20 minutes
Cook Time: 25 minutes
Total Time: 45 minutes

Ingredients

1 pound of lean ground beef (85% or higher)
1 box (12 ounces) of Barilla Gluten Free Rotini Pasta
½ package (8 ounces) of cream cheese, softened
1 jar (24-28 ounces) of your favorite pasta sauce
1 onion, minced
1 teaspoon of Italian seasoning
½ teaspoon of red pepper flakes
2 cloves of garlic, minced

½ cup of shredded mozzarella cheese

Directions

Preheat oven to 350 degrees Fahrenheit.

Bring a large pot of water to a boil.

Add pasta to water, stirring occasionally, cooking for about 12 minutes or until the pasta is just becoming soft to the bite (al dente). Drain pasta and return it to the pot.

Mix in cream cheese with pasta, so that it melts and mixes thoroughly.

Stir Italian seasoning, pasta sauce, and red pepper flakes into the pasta and cream cheese mixture.

Heat the ground beef over medium heat in a large skillet for just 2 to 3 minutes, then add the onion and garlic and continue cooking until the ground beef is browned.

Stir the beef/onion/garlic mixture into the pasta mixture to combine the two.

Pour everything into a 3 quart casserole dish and top with mozzarella cheese.

Bake until the cheese melts and is bubbling, approximately 5 to 10 minutes.

Serve and enjoy!

Meaty Roll Ups

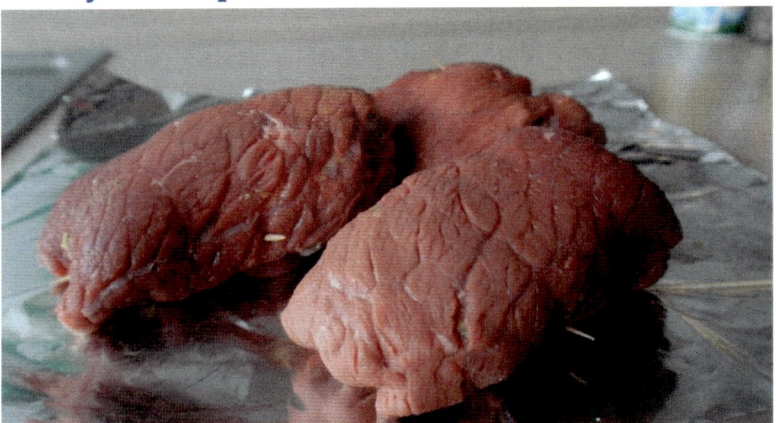

I added this dish to the beef section because while it has more chicken than beef, the flavor of the smoked beef overtakes the chicken, so you remember it as a beef dish more than anything. You probably don't have apricot jam just lying around, but trust me, it is worth the special trip to the store to make this wonderful finger food!

Preparation Time: 10 minutes
Cook Time: 25 minutes
Total Time: 35 minutes

Ingredients
½ cup of Ketchup
½ cup of mayonnaise
½ cup of apricot jam
3 skinless, boneless chicken breast halves, pounded thin
12 slices of smoked beef

Directions
Preheat oven to 350 degrees Fahrenheit.

Trim the fat from the smoked beef, and place a piece over each chicken breast slice, then roll. Fasten with toothpicks to keep it all together.

Place the rolls seam side down in a 9x12 inch baking dish.

Mix together ketchup, mayonnaise and jam until thoroughly combined into a sauce.

Pour the sauce over the rolls.

Bake uncovered for 20 to 25 minutes.

Serve and enjoy!

Simple, Amazing Rib Roast

Rib roast can be expensive if it is not on sale, but when you do splurge, it can be absolutely amazing if cooked right! This recipe has just 4 ingredients, but it does take 5 hours to cook, so plan ahead! Between the time needed and the expense, this is a dish best served at a family gathering such as Christmas or even Easter dinner. Don't let the time needed scare you though – it's almost all about just letting it sit in the oven!

Preparation Time: 5 minutes
Cook Time: 5 hours
Total Time: 5 hours, 5 minutes

Ingredients

1 standing beef rib roast, 5 pounds
2 teaspoons of salt
1 teaspoon of ground black pepper
1 teaspoon of garlic powder

Directions

To start, let the roast sit at room for temperature (i.e. out of the refrigerator) for at least an hour.

Preheat the oven to 375 degrees Fahrenheit.

Combine all spices in a small dish.

Place the roast on a rack, in a roasting pan, with the fatty side up and the rib side down.

Rub the spices all over the roast, spreading them as evenly as possible.

Roast for 1 hour in the oven.

Turn the oven off, leaving the roast inside for 3 hours. Do not open the oven during this time, as heat will escape.

After the 3 hours are up, turn the oven back on to 375 degrees Fahrenheit.

Roast for 30-40 minutes, just long enough until reheated, or an internal temperature of approximately 145 degrees Fahrenheit.

Remove the roast from the oven and allow to rest for 10 minutes.

Carve, serve, and enjoy!

Cumin and Garlic Leg of Lamb

Leg of lamb, just like the rib roast, is a dish best served at a family gathering such as Christmas or Easter dinner, or just to celebrate something special. It is more expensive to buy a leg of lamb butterflied, boned and trimmed at the butcher, but it is well worth the time saved to have that already done. Enjoy your time with family and/or friends while this beauty is slow cooking!

Preparation Time: 1 hour, 25 minutes
Cook Time: 50-60 minutes
Total Time: 2 hours, 40 minutes to 2 hours, 50 minutes

Ingredients
1 (8 pound) leg of lamb, boned and butterflied to an even

thickness, 4 ½ to 5 ½ pounds trimmed weight, fell with most fat removed
¼ cup of olive oil
8 cloves of garlic, minced
1 lemon, juiced
2 ½ teaspoons salt
1 teaspoon pepper
2 tablespoons of ground cumin
1 tablespoon of dried oregano
Optional: Minced fresh parsley or mint

Directions

Mix the olive oil, garlic, salt, pepper, cumin and oregano together, spread evenly on both sides of the lamb, then let sit for an hour to get the meat up to room temperature.

Preheat broiler on oven to high for about 10 minutes, adjusting the oven rack to the upper-middle position.

Place lamb cut-side up on a large wire rack set over a foil lined roasting pan.

Broil for roughly 8 minutes, or until the surface browns evenly.

Turn the lamb over and broil on the other side for about 8 minutes, or until the surface is evenly browned.

Turn off broiler, remove lamb and let it rest for 10 minutes.

Heat the oven to 325 degrees Fahrenheit.

Put a meat thermometer into the thickest part of the lamb (you will need to know its internal temperature).

Place the lamb back in the oven and cook for 50 minutes to 1 hour, or until the thermometer reads about 140 degrees. You will need to check it every few minutes after it has been in for about 30 minutes.

Remove lamb from oven, and immediately squeeze the lemon's juice all over it, then sprinkle it with the fresh herbs if you chose to use them.

Carve (going across the grain), then drizzle with juices from the roasting pan.

Serve and enjoy!

Rosemary Roast Leg of Lamb

Unlike the previous lamb recipe, this one marinates overnight, so it takes far less steps to prepare. Not only does it take less time, but allowing the seasoning to soak while you sleep gets the flavors deep into the meat and it is downright delicious.

Preparation Time: 15 minutes
Cook Time: 1 hour, 20 minutes
Total Time: 1 hour, 35 minutes

Ingredients

1 (5 pounds) whole leg of lamb
¼ cup of honey
3 cloves of garlic, minced
2 tablespoons of Dijon mustard
2 tablespoons of chopped fresh rosemary
1 teaspoon of lemon zest
1 teaspoon of sea salt
1 teaspoon of freshly ground black pepper

Directions

Marinade: Combine the honey, mustard, rosemary, ground black pepper, lemon zest and garlic in a small bowl. Apply all over the lamb, then cover and let marinate in the refrigerator overnight.

Preheat oven to 450 degrees Fahrenheit.

Place leg of lamb on a rack in a roasting pan, and season evenly with salt. Insert an internal thermometer into the thickest part of the meat.

Bake for 20 minutes, then reduce heat to 400 degrees Farenheit. Allow lamb to roast at the lowered temperature for 55 to 60 minutes for medium rare (longer if you would like it more well done). The internal temperature should be at least 145 degrees.

Remove lamb from oven, and allow it to rest for about 10 minutes.

Carve (going across the grain), then drizzle with juices from the roasting pan.

Serve and enjoy!

Impossibly Easy Breakfast Bake

Bisquick's Gluten Free mix lets you create a delicious, satisfying breakfast casserole without any wheat. This dish is cheesy, hot and yummy – perfect for a breakfast with many people! You can also freeze individual pieces and heat them up later, in case the recipe makes too much for you to eat all at once.

Preparation Time: 20 minutes
Cook Time: 35 minutes
Total Time: 55 minutes

Ingredients

¾ cup of Bisquick Gluten Free mix
1 pound (16 ounces) of pork sausage
3 cups of frozen hash browns
2 cups of shredded cheddar cheese
2 cups of whole milk
6 eggs
1 medium red bell pepper, chopped
1 medium yellow onion, chopped
¼ teaspoon of ground black pepper

Directions

Preheat oven to 400 degrees Fahrenheit.

Spray a 9 x 13 inch baking dish with cooking spray of your choice.

In a large skillet, cook the sausage, onion and bell pepper over medium heat until sausage is browned. Drain.

Combine the sausage/onion/pepper mixture with the hash browns and 1 ½ cups of the cheese, then pour into the greased baking dish.

In a separate bowl, combine the Bisquick Gluten Free mix, eggs, milk and pepper until well blended. Pour over everything already in the baking dish.

Bake for 30-35 minutes, or until a toothpick inserted in the center of the casserole comes out clean.

Once cooked, sprinkle the remaining ½ cup of cheese and then continue to bake for roughly 3 minutes, just long enough for the extra cheese to melt.

Let stand for 5 minutes to cool.

Serve and enjoy!

Italian Sausage and Spaghetti Squash Casserole

This dish is given a wonderful zing by using Italian sausage, Italian spiced tomatoes, onion, and 3 cloves of garlic. The spaghetti squash does add a bit of extra work, but if you'd rather not use it you can substitute it with Barilla Gluten Free spaghetti, boiled and drained.

Preparation Time: 20 minutes
Cook Time: 1 hour, 40 minutes
Total Time: 2 hours

Ingredients
1 (3 pound) of spaghetti squash, halved and seeded
1 pound (16 ounces) of Italian sausage
1 cup of shredded mozzarella cheese
1 small yellow onion, diced
1 rib of celery, diced
1 small carrot, diced

3 cloves of garlic, pressed
1 can (15 ounces) of diced tomatoes with basil, garlic, and oregano
1 ½ cups of chicken broth
½ small can (6 ounces) of tomato paste

Directions

Preheat oven to 400 degrees Fahrenheit.

Line a baking sheet with parchment paper, then lay the prepared squash cut side down on it.

Bake squash for about 25 minutes, or until just starting to soften.

Reduce oven temperature to 350 degrees Fahrenheit and continue baking until the squash can be easily pierced with a knife, about 25 more minutes.

Remove squash from oven and cool until it can be easily handled with bare hands.

Brown sausage in a large skillet for approximately 5 minutes, then transfer the sausage to a bowl, WITHOUT draining the fat from the sausage.

Cook the onion, carrot and celery in the sausage fat within the skillet until the onion is starting to turn clear and everything is beginning to soften, roughly 5 minutes.

Stir the cooked sausage, canned tomatoes, tomato paste, chicken broth, and garlic into the skillet. Simmer until everything is combined, roughly 15 minutes.

Using a fork, scrape the insides of both squash halves into spaghetti strands.

Transfer the squash strands to a greased 9" x 13" casserole dish.

Spoon the contents of the skillet over the spaghetti squash strands, then stir to combine everything.

Top the contents of the casserole dish with mozzarella cheese.

Bake until the cheese is bubbling and the dish is an overall golden brown, roughly 25 minutes.

Serve and enjoy!

Bacon and Egg Quiche Lorraine

This quiche Lorraine recipe uses almond meal for the crust, and is filled with a rich, flavorful mixture of eggs, half-and-half, bacon, and swiss cheese. A single slice will probably be enough to fill you up, but it makes plenty, so dig in!

Preparation Time: 20 minutes
Cook Time: 55 minutes
Total Time: 1 hour, 15 minutes

Ingredients

Crust:
2 cups of almond meal
½ cup (4 ounces) of melted butter
1 tablespoon of garlic, minced
½ teaspoon of sea salt
1/8 teaspoon of ground white pepper

Filling:
8 slices of thick cut bacon, cooked and crumbled
1 cup (8 ounces) of shredded Swiss cheese
1 cup (8 ounces) of half-and-half

5 large eggs
½ teaspoon of sea salt
¼ teaspoon of ground white pepper
A pinch of ground nutmeg

Directions

Preheat oven to 350 degrees Fahrenheit.

Mix almond meal, garlic, sea salt, 1/8 teaspoon of white pepper, and melted butter together until you form the dough into a ball.

Press the dough into a 9 inch pie pan until it covers the entire bottom and partially up the sides.

Bake the pie pan with the crust for 20 minutes in the preheated oven. Continually check the crust and when it begins to puff up, press it back down with a spoon. Remove the crust from the oven when it is lightly browned.

Using a whisk, mix the eggs, half-and-half, sea salt, nutmeg, and ¼ teaspoon of white pepper in a large bowl until thoroughly combined.

Evenly sprinkle the crumbled bacon over the bottom of the cooked pie crust, then cover the bacon with the shredded swiss cheese.

Pour the egg mixture over the swiss cheese in the pie pan.

Bake for about 35 minutes, or until a toothpick inserted in the center comes out clean.

Allow pie to cool for 5 to 10 minutes so that it can "set" in the middle.

Serve and enjoy!

Italian Seasoned Pork Tenderloin

The Italian spices used to coat the tenderloin in this recipe help to keep the pork from drying out, and they give it amazing flavor. The breadcrumbs are completely optional (and not pictured above, as I don't normally use them) but can be a nice touch of added texture for those who desire it. Glutino, Panko, Schar, and Kinnikinnick all make gluten free breadcrumbs – you just may have to shop online to find them as they might not be available in your local grocery store, but Walmart should at least have Glutino.

Preparation Time: 10 minutes
Cook Time: 35 minutes
Total Time: 55 minutes

Ingredients

2 pork tenderloins
2 cups of gluten free breadcrumbs
½ cup (4 ounces) of olive oil
1 teaspoon of dried oregano

1 teaspoon of dried basil
1 teaspoon of dried rosemary
1 teaspoon of garlic powder

Directions

Preheat oven to 425 degrees Fahrenheit.

Line a baking sheet with non-stick aluminum foil.

Combine bread crumbs, olive oil, rosemary, basil, oregano, and garlic in a large zip-top plastic bag. Add the pork tenderloin to the bag, seal it, and then shake vigorously until the pork is thoroughly coated.

Place tenderloin on baking sheet, then bake for about 35 minutes (the internal temperature should be at least 145 degrees Fahrenheit).

Let pork rest for 10 minutes after removing from oven.

Cut into ½" think slices, serve and enjoy!

Bacon and Three Cheese Macaroni

The wonder of rice pasta becoming mainstream is that now we can indulge ourselves like we are kids again! I normally use Barilla pasta, but any rice pasta will do. What makes this particular macaroni and cheese recipe special (as there are several in this book) is the three "grown up" cheeses, heavy whipping cream, and of course the BACON!

Preparation Time: 15 minutes
Cook Time: 30 minutes
Total Time: 45 minutes

Ingredients

1 box (16 ounces) of Barilla Gluten Free Elbows Pasta
8 slices of thick cut bacon, cooked and chopped
2 cups (16 ounces) of heavy whipping cream
1 cup (8 ounces) of shredded Cheddar cheese
1 cup (8 ounces) of shredded Fontina cheese
1 cup (8 ounces) of shredded Gouda cheese
Salt to taste
Black pepper to taste

Directions

Preheat oven to 350 degrees Fahrenheit.

Grease a 9" x 13" baking dish.

Bring a large pot to a boil. Cook elbow macaroni, stirring occasionally, until cooked but still firm to the bite, roughly 8 minutes.

Drain the pasta and set it aside.

Stir cream, salt and pepper in a large saucepan over medium heat.

Add 2 tablespoons of each cheese together in a separate bowl and set aside.

Stir in the rest of the cheeses with the cream until completely melted into a smooth cheese sauce, roughly 5 minutes. Stir frequently while cooking. Remove saucepan from heat.

Mix the pasta and cheese sauce together until evenly combined, then fold in the chopped bacon.

Pour the entire mixture into the baking dish, then top with the remaining 2 tablespoons of each cheese (6 tablespoons total).

Bake until the cheese is melted and bubbling, roughly 15 minutes.

Serve and enjoy!

Mexican Chorizo Bake

Don't let the amount of ingredients in this dish scare you, because the taste is out of this world and it takes less than 20 minutes to prepare. Chorizo and ground beef are the big protein here, but then you add in black beans, cream cheese, and guacamole, and it becomes a powerhouse of a meal. The many spices used give it such a flavor that you'll be sure to make this recipe a staple in your home! The recipe as it stands is completely grain free, but you can also use it as taco filling or nacho topping.

Preparation Time: 15 minutes
Cook Time: 55 minutes
Total Time: 1 hour, 10 minutes

Ingredients

1 package (2 pounds) of frozen hash browns
½ pound (8 ounces) of lean ground beef
½ pound (8 ounces) of Mexican chorizo, casing removed and meat crumbled
1 cup (8 ounces) of frozen corn
½ package (8 ounces) of cream cheese, softened
1 cup (8 ounces) of shredded cheddar cheese

1 cup (8 ounces) of prepared guacamole
½ cup (4 ounces) of chopped yellow onion
1 can (15 ounces) of black beans, drained and rinsed
1 can (14.5 ounces) of canned, diced tomatoes
1 tablespoon of olive oil
1 tablespoon of chili powder
1 tablespoon of butter
1 ½ teaspoons of ground cumin
1 teaspoon of salt
1 teaspoon of smoked paprika
½ teaspoon of ground coriander
½ teaspoon of ground black pepper
Shredded lettuce for garnish

Directions

Preheat oven to 350 degrees Fahrenheit.

Heat the olive oil in a large skillet over medium-high heat, then stir in ground beef, chorizo and onion until the meat is browned, roughly 5 to 7 minutes.

Sprinkle the meat mixture with the cumin, paprika, salt, coriander, chili powder, and black pepper.

Add corn, beans and tomatoes to the mixture, then stir and cook everything until heated through, roughly 5 minutes.

Pour the entire contents of the skillet into a greased 2 quart baking dish.

Place cream cheese and butter in a microwave safe bowl, microwave for about 1 minute or until both are melted. Stir the mixture until it is smooth, then spread it evenly over the contents of the baking dish.

Evenly place hash browns on top of the cream cheese and butter mixture, then top everything with the Cheddar cheese.

Bake until the cheese is melted and the potatoes are brown, roughly 30 to 40 minutes.

Serve with the shredded lettuce and guacamole, and enjoy!

Sausage and Pepperoni Pizza Bake

Using Barilla Gluten Free Rotini pasta for this one-dish bake gives you a pizza that you eat with a fork! Ingredients can be added or omitted depending on how you usually take your pizza. Just make sure to include the cream cheese, it makes things oh-so-creamy and moist while also helping to hold everything together.

Preparation Time: 15 minutes
Cook Time: 55 minutes
Total Time: 1 hour, 10 minutes

Ingredients

1 box (16 ounces) of Barilla Gluten Free Rotini pasta
1 pound (16 ounces) of Italian sausage
4 ounces of sliced pepperoni, or more if desired for topping
1 jar (24 ounces) of old fashioned/traditional pasta sauce
½ sweet onion, diced
2 cups of shredded mozzarella cheese
2 ounces of cream cheese, softened
½ teaspoon Italian seasoning

Directions

Preheat oven to 350 degrees Fahrenheit.

Grease a 9" x 13" baking dish.

Boil the gluten free pasta in a large pot as the directions indicate.

While you are waiting on the pasta to cook, brown the sausage in a large skillet over medium heat until it is just slightly pink (not all the way browned). Add onion, then cook both the meat and onion together until the onion is clear and the meat is fully browned.

Add the pepperoni, cream cheese, and pasta sauce to the skillet and cook over low heat until the cheese has melted and everything is thoroughly combined.

Once the pasta is cooked, drain it then return it to the pot. Stir the meat/sauce mixture into the pasta until everything is coated.

Add half of the new pasta mixture to the baking dish, and top with half of the mozzarella cheese.

Spread the rest of the pasta mixture over the layer of cheese, then top that with the rest of the mozzarella cheese.

Sprinkle Italian seasoning evenly over the dish's surface and top with some pepperoni.

Bake the dish until the cheese has melted, approximately 15 minutes.

Let cool for 10 minutes, serve and enjoy!

Simple Tuna Noodle Casserole

This classic comfort dish is something just about every American can remember from their childhood, and for good reason: it is a quick, protein packed dinner that is very cost efficient, so perfect if you have a family. I prefer Barilla brand, but any gluten free pasta will do, in any shape. Glutino, Panko, Schar, and Kinnikinnick all make gluten free breadcrumbs – you just may have to shop online to find them as they might not be available in your local grocery store.

Preparation Time: 25 minutes
Cook Time: 10 minutes
Total Time: 35 minutes

Ingredients

2 6-ounce cans of tuna, drained
2 cups (16 ounces) of heavy cream
3 cups of shredded Cheddar cheese
½ cup (4 ounces) of gluten free bread crumbs
1 box (16 ounces) of Barilla Gluten Free Rotini pasta
1 cup (8 ounces) of yellow onion, diced
1 cup (8 ounces) of frozen peas, thawed

1 10-ounce package of baby spinach
4 tablespoons of olive oil
Salt to taste
Black pepper to taste

Directions

Preheat oven to 400 degrees Fahrenheit.

Bring a large pot of water to a boil and grease a 9" x 13" baking dish.

While you wait for the water to boil, add 2 tablespoons of olive oil to a large skillet and cook onions over high heat until they are just turning clear, roughly 5 minutes.

Adjust the heat for the skillet to medium and then add the spinach and peas, cooking until the spinach wilts, then add the cream, stirring frequently.

Stir in salt and pepper and bring the entire mixture up to a simmer.

Gently fold in 2 cups of the Cheddar cheese to the skillet. Remove skillet from heat.

If the water is now boiling, add the pasta and cook according to the box's instructions.

Drain the pasta, add the sauce in the skillet, then add in the drained tuna, mixing everything until fully combined.

Place the entire mixture in the greased baking dish and top with the remaining 1 cup of cheese.

Combine the remaining olive oil, the gluten free bread crumbs, and some salt and pepper into a small bowl, then evenly spread this mixture over the very top of the baking dish's contents.

Bake until the bread becomes crunchy and golden brown, roughly 10 minutes.

Allow dish to cool for 10 minutes, then serve and enjoy!

Garlic Baked Tilapia

Tilapia is a mild fish, so this recipe is perfect because it jazzes it right up with an overnight marinade! Be sure to buy the tilapia filleted from the fish counter at your grocery store, because that will make the preparation time for this dish only 5 minutes.

Preparation Time: 5 minutes
Cook Time: 30 minutes
Total Time: 35 minutes

Ingredients
4 4-ounce fresh tilapia fillets
1 yellow onion, chopped
4 cloves of garlic, crushed
3 tablespoons of olive oil
¼ teaspoon of cayenne pepper

Directions
The night before you are going to make this fish, rub both sides of each fillet with the crushed garlic, then put them in a shallow ceramic or glass dish. Drizzle olive oil over the top of the fish

until they are coated, then place the chopped onion on top. Cover the dish and place in the refrigerator overnight.

When you are ready to cook the fish, preheat the oven to 350 degrees Fahrenheit.

Place all 4 fillets into a 9" x 13" baking dish, being careful to keep all the olive oil, onion and garlic in place.

Sprinkle the tops of the fish with the cayenne pepper (alternatively, you can use white pepper if you don't like cayenne).

Bake for 30 minutes.

Serve and enjoy!

Individual Portobello Pizzas

Individual pizzas are always a great option for families because each person gets to customize their own. The recipe below is for a typical pepperoni pizza, but like any pizza, go crazy adding any toppings you desire! The fact that these only take 10 minutes to prepare makes them that much more fun – if anyone decides they want another, it's all too easy to make more! Just make sure you adjust the recipe amounts if you are planning to make more than 4.

Preparation Time: 10 minutes
Cook Time: 20 minutes
Total Time: 30 minutes

Ingredients

4 large Portobello mushroom cups, gills removed
2 cups (16 ounces) of fresh mozzarella cheese, sliced thin
½ cup of fresh basil, chopped
3 tablespoons of extra virgin olive oil
4 ounces of sliced pepperoni
Salt to taste
Black ground pepper to taste

Directions

Preheat oven to 375 degrees Fahrenheit.

Line a baking sheet with non-stick aluminum foil.

Place the mushroom cups, top side down, on the baking sheet. Drizzle olive oil over the cups and season with salt and pepper.

Layer ¾ of the mozzarella cheese onto the mushrooms, then top with basil and any other vegetables you have chosen to include.

Place the remaining cheese on top of the mushrooms, then top with pepperoni slices.

Bake until the mushrooms are tender and the cheese is melted, roughly 20 to 25 minutes.

Allow to cool for 5 minutes, serve and enjoy!

Quinoa Crusted Quiche

There are a lot of "crustless" quinoa quiches out there, however this one has a crust MADE from quinoa, albeit a thin one. Do not let that fool you though, just because it is thin does not mean it is fragile! The most readily available quinoa flour is from a brand called Bob's Red Mill, which can be found at most grocery chains.

Preparation Time: 20 minutes
Cook Time: 45 minutes
Total Time: 1 hour, 5 minutes

Ingredients

7 large eggs
1 ¼ cups of quinoa flour
1 ½ cups of chopped broccoli
2 large green onions, chopped
2 cups of chopped mushrooms
½ cup of half-and-half
2/3 cups of shredded Cheddar cheese
1/3 cups of butter, room temperature
½ teaspoon of garlic salt
2 tablespoons of water

Directions

Preheat oven to 350 degrees Fahrenheit.

Grease a 9 inch pie pan with butter.

Cook mushrooms in a dry skillet over medium heat, stirring frequently until they are soft and have released their liquid, roughly 10 minutes. Remove from heat.

Using a whisk, mix the eggs and half-and-half together in a bowl, then stir in the Cheddar cheese, broccoli, green onions, garlic salt, and the cooked mushrooms. Place this filling in the refrigerator.

Mix the quinoa flour and the butter in a bowl until it forms small clumps, then stir water into the mixture until it becomes a dough. Add more water, ½ teaspoon at a time, if the dough is too dry.

Press the dough into the prepared pie dish, flattening along the bottom and pushing up along the sides to form a pie crust.

Pour the chilled filling into the crust.

Bake the pie dish until a toothpick inserted in the middle comes out clean, roughly 35 minutes.

Let cool for 5 minutes, serve and enjoy!

Quinoa Meatless Frittatas

These little egg and veggie muffins are so versatile, you can have them as a meal or as a side, and you can eat them hot or cold. I usually double the recipe because as it stands this recipe only makes 6 muffins, and I like to have some extra that I can heat up for later! If you don't want these to be vegetarian, simply remove the beans from the recipe and add in your favorite meat, such as ham.

Preparation Time: 15 minutes
Cook Time: 45 minutes
Total Time: 1 hour

Ingredients

1 cup of quinoa
1 ½ cups of water
1 ¼ cups of shredded zucchini
1 cup of shredded mozzarella cheese
2 eggs
2 egg whites
6 tablespoons of shredded Parmesan cheese, divided
1 teaspoon of olive oil
2 tablespoons of fresh rosemary, chopped
¾ cup of black beans, drained and rinsed
¼ teaspoon of ground white pepper

Directions

Mix together quinoa, water and olive oil in a saucepan, and bring to a boil.

Stir rosemary into the quinoa mixture, then reduce heat to medium-low, cover and simmer until the quinoa is tender and the water has been absorbed, roughly 15 to 20 minutes.

Preheat oven to 400 degrees Fahrenheit. Grease or line 6 muffin cups.

Combine the quinoa mixture, mozzarella cheese, black beans, zucchini, eggs, egg whites, white pepper, and ¼ cup of the Parmesan cheese in a large bowl.

Spoon the new mixture into each muffin cup, roughly 2/3 of the way full, then top with the remaining Parmesan cheese.

Bake until the muffins are set in the middle and the edges are golden brown, roughly 25 to 30 minutes.

Cool for 5 minutes until removing the frittatas from the muffin cups.

Serve and enjoy!

Spicy Macaroni and Cheese

This is a different take on a "grown up mac and cheese" – a spicy one! Not only does this recipe use pepperjack cheese, it also has minced jalapeno peppers mixed in. Add to that heavy cream and milk, and you have yourself a fiery, creamy, yummy dish that could be its own meal or a side. If the jalapeno pepper is too spicy for you, simply toss out the seeds and just use the flesh of the pepper.

Preparation Time: 25 minutes
Cook Time: 15 minutes
Total Time: 40 minutes

Ingredients
1 (12 ounce) box of Barilla Gluten Free Elbow pasta

2 cups of heavy cream
2 cups of organic milk
1 pound (16 ounces) of shredded pepperjack cheese
1 small fresh jalapeno pepper, minced
4 egg yolks, lightly beaten
1 tablespoon of corn starch
Salt and pepper to taste

Directions

Preheat oven to 400 degrees Fahrenheit, and start a large pot of water to boil.

Grease a 9" x 9" baking dish.

Cook pasta 2 minutes shorter than the recommended cooking time on the box.

In a small sauce pan, heat the milk and cream until it begins to simmer.

Mix the corn starch and 2 tablespoons of water in a small bowl until it creates a slurry.

Mix the corn starch slurry in with the cream and milk until it thickens, then add in the salt, pepper, and minced jalapeno.

Slowly add ¾ of the cheese into the sauce, whisking frequently until smooth.

Stir in the undercooked pasta to the mixture and let everything sit for roughly 5 minutes.

Stir in the egg yolks, then pour everything into the 9" x 9" baking dish.

Bake until bubbling and slightly caramelized on top, roughly 15 minutes.

Remove from oven and let stand for several minutes to cool.

Serve and enjoy!

Italian 3 Cheese Eggplant Lasagna

This is one of the most flavorful lasagnas I have made to date. The oregano, basil, garlic, onion powder, and the 3 cheeses (ricotta, Romano, and mozzarella) come together in – if you'll excuse the cliché – a symphony of flavor. One slice should be plenty to fill you up, but if not, never fear, for this dish makes plenty to go around!

Preparation Time: 40 minutes
Cook Time: 45 minutes
Total Time: 1 hour, 25 minutes

Ingredients

2 eggplants, sliced lengthwise into ¼" thick slices
2 large eggs
½ cup (4 ounces) of freshly grated Romano cheese
1 (15 ounce) container of Ricotta cheese
1 cup (8 ounces) of shredded mozzarella cheese
1 can (28 ounces) of crushed tomatoes

1 can (6 ounces) of tomato paste
1 yellow onion, diced
1 cup (8 ounces) of frozen, chopped spinach
1 cup (8 ounces) of shredded carrots
2 tablespoons of salt
2 tablespoons of canola oil
1 teaspoon of dried oregano
1 teaspoon of dried basil
2 teaspoons of garlic powder
2 teaspoon of onion powder
1 tablespoon of olive oil
1 teaspoon of olive oil
Salt to taste
Ground black pepper to taste

Directions

Salt both sides of the eggplant slices, then layer them in a 9" x 13" baking dish with paper towels between each layer.

Place a smaller baking dish on top of the eggplant slices, and fill it with several sealed heavy food cans to weight it down. Let sit for at least an hour, until the paper towels are visibly moist.

Rinse the eggplant slices under running water, then pat dry with paper towels.

Heat a large skillet to medium heat, then put in 2 tablespoons of canola oil.

Cook both sides of the eggplant slices until they are slightly browned, roughly 5 minutes per side. Set all of the cooked eggplant aside.

To create the tomato sauce, combine the crushed tomatoes,

tomato paste, basil, oregano, 1 teaspoon of garlic powder, 1 tablespoon of olive oil, 1 teaspoon of onion powder, salt, and black pepper in a small bowl. Set aside.

Heat 1 teaspoon of olive oil in a skillet over medium heat, stir onion in the skillet until it is clear, roughly 5 minutes.

Add the frozen spinach and carrots to the onion in the skillet, cook until everything becomes dry, roughly 5 to 8 minutes. Set aside to cool.

Mix together the ricotta cheese, eggs, Romano cheese, 1 teaspoon of onion powder, 1 teaspoon of garlic powder, and ½ teaspoon of salt in a separate bowl.

Spoon the cooled carrot/spinach/onion mixture into the ricotta mixture until thoroughly combined.

Preheat oven to 350 degrees Fahrenheit.

Pour a thin layer of the tomato sauce into a 9" x 13" baking dish, just covering the bottom of the dish.

Place half of the eggplant slices in a layer on top of the tomato sauce.

Spread half the ricotta cheese mixture on top of the eggplant layer.

Pour another layer of tomato sauce, then put the remaining eggplant slices on top of it, then the remaining ricotta mixture on the very top.

Finally, put one last layer of tomato sauce over everything, then evenly sprinkle mozzarella cheese over the entire top.

Bake until the mozzarella cheese is browned, roughly 45 minutes.

Let cool for 10 minutes, then serve and enjoy!

Lasagna Style Zucchini Parmesan Bake

This lasagna-type recipe, unlike the last one, is quite simple and easy. It uses zucchini instead of pasta, which is easily sliced length-wise and then browned in a skillet, no baking, rinsing, or patting dry required. For simplicity's sake there are only two kinds of cheeses and only salt and pepper for spices, but by all means feel free to dress this one up however you'd like! Throw in some sausage or ground beef, add in some Italian spices, include some onion for a bit of extra zing. I must say though, if you like zucchini, this recipe is pretty darn tasty all by itself.

Preparation Time: 30 minutes
Cook Time: 15 minutes
Total Time: 45 minutes

Ingredients

4 zucchini, thinly sliced length-wise
1 (16 ounce) jar of marinara sauce
½ cup (4 ounces) of grated Parmesan cheese
1 cup (8 ounces) of shredded mozzarella cheese
Salt to taste
Pepper to taste
Cooking spray

Directions

Preheat oven to 350 degrees Fahrenheit.

Spray a 9" x 13" baking dish with cooking spray.

Use salt and pepper on both sides of the zucchini slices to evenly coat them.

Spray cooking spray in a large skillet, then cook zucchini over medium-heat until slightly browned, about 2 to 3 minutes for each side.

Spread ½ cup of the marinara sauce in the baking dish. Layer zucchini slices, overlapping a bit, on top of the marinara sauce layer.

Spread ½ cup of marinara sauce over the zucchini layer, then top with ¼ cup of Parmesan cheese and ½ cup of mozzarella cheese.

Continue by layering more zucchini, then ½ cup of marinara, then ¼ cup of Parmesan cheese, and then the remaining ½ cup of mozzarella cheese finally on the very top.

Bake until the cheese is melted, about 10 minutes.

Allow to cool for roughly 10 minutes, then serve and enjoy!

Made in the USA
Monee, IL
18 December 2023